Life Is Your Song: Discover Your Voice!

RESET your inner compass, UNDERSTAND who you really are, and FIND your place in the world!

Tonya H. Ware

#LIFEisyoursong

The following resources were used in the writing of this book:
http://topnonprofits.com/examples/nonprofit-mission-statements/
http://www.thefreedictionary.com
http://www.merriam-webster.com
Copyright © 2014 Tonya H. Ware
All rights reserved.
ISBN-10: 0692282599
ISBN-13: 978-0692282595 (The Success House Press)

Dedications

To the following persons who directly or indirectly inspired me to write this book. You made an impression upon me that will never be erased! From the bottom of my heart, thank you!

Adrian D. Ware, LL Cool J, Tammie Sykes, Jessie J. Johnson, Dr. Bill Winston, Dr. Douglas Wolfe, Steve Harrison, Susan Boyle, Marco Aguilar, T.D. Jakes, and Mike, the bus driver for the Renaissance Airport Hotel in Philadelphia, Pennsylvania.

A special thank you goes to Geoffrey Berwind, Tamra Nashman, Martha Bullen and Mary Giuseffi for their guidance and support in writing this book.

Table of Contents

Personal Action Guide:

This book includes a personal action guide at the end of each key principle to assist you in reaching your fullest potential! *As a composer creates a song, we have the power to create the life we desire.*

Introduction

Most of us, at some point, have been through tremendous pain and trauma that have derailed us and taken our lives completely off course. The result of such encounters often leaves you with a "mis-calibrated" inner compass that renders you "lost" even though you may appear to know where you are going. I lost my direction too.

In December 2006, after pushing my body for several years, I got up early to prepare for another productive day at work and *suddenly died* in my master bathroom after having had a violent grand mal seizure. Through the seizure, I could hear Adrian, my husband, praying and fighting for my life. Toward the end, I remember feeling my spirit leave my body. For me, after this, there was silence. I was gone. My husband was relentless in not "letting me go." To this day, he tells me he prayed his most desperate prayer on that day, and miraculously I revived. When I came back from death, the journey began. I started an extensive series of medical tests, examinations, and doctor appointments that all came back with negative diagnoses. I was declared totally disabled.

I went from being a corporate mega-million-dollar producer who had just recorded my debut album, *Tonya Ware–The Voice*, to living as a virtual shut in, only able to leave my house a few times a week.

I would muster enough strength to go to church, but the rest of the week, I was home in bed or on the sofa, drained of vitality and strength. The unprovoked fainting and seizures continually left me feeling "washed out" and depleted of energy.

Worst of all, as the time moved on and one year led to another year and yet another year, I lost my inner voice. Life was so painful that I wanted to give up and die. I felt like I was living in slow motion. Often, I felt as though what was happening was unreal. The real Tonya was strong, bold, and fearless. I was a winner. Whatever I wanted, I went after it, and I got it. Now, I was in another place. Physical illnesses not only works against the body, but in a prolonged state, physical illnesses can greatly affect your confidence, thoughts, and your ability to function at an optimum emotional level.

So, for more than six, long years, I fought desperately to recover my health, my life, and my strength. In the process of getting my life back, I realized something very key. I not only died a natural death, but I had allowed sickness, anger, and depression to cause me to die a second death. The real me, my inner voice–my spirit– during those years, ceased to exist as well. My sense was that I was empty and void inside. This illness took my ability to drive, do any vigorous activities, tolerate heat and sudden cold, along with many other limitations. It got to a place where the list of what I could *not* do was longer than the list of things that I could do. I walked around, most days, feeling like someone's hand was over my mouth. I felt like a hostage in my own body and in my own house. I was screaming on the inside, but no one could hear my cries. I felt I was in a downward spiral, over which I had no control. My feet lost their foundation. I lost my passion, my way, my voice!

Here is more of my story…

I am a native of Key West, Florida, and I began singing at the age of six. My first public audience (outside of my church) was while I was in high school. I would accompany my dad and other clergy when they went to minister to inmates in local jails. As soon as I opened my mouth to share my music with them, the inmates rushed to the front bars to hear me sing. I became known as the "little girl with *the voice.*"

After graduating from high school with honors, I enrolled and graduated from Mississippi State University. There, I joined a noted campus choir and traveled extensively, performing. It was during those days that my gift to sing and perform in front of large audiences was developed.

After graduating from college, I landed an amazing position. For more than twelve years, I focused my attention on my career, a benefits and retirement planner for a Fortune 500 company. Life for me was really great at this point. Growing up very poor, I had vowed that I would work hard to be successful. My career had become my life, and working sixteen-to eighteen-hour days was my norm. The hours were long, and I had to drive, sometimes over a hundred miles one way, to my assignment, but I absolutely loved it. Life was good!

In early 2006, I recorded my debut album, *Tonya Ware–The Voice.* My single release, "Put My Hand in Yours," written by the legendary Marvin Winans, stood up to and still stands up to some of today's "hottest" music in both mainstream and Christian markets worldwide. So I was working my benefits and retirement planner position daily, and my weekends were consumed with recording music and operating as the musical director at my church.

Just as everything seemed to be coming together for me, I experienced heart and other health problems. I became so tired of being stuck and prodded at every doctor's visit that even my veins in my arms stopped showing up. Every part of me was tired. Over the years of being treated, in addition to losing my inner voice and feeling lost, I slowly developed a hole within my soul. Fear of the future and profound sadness became my daily meditation. I began to consider myself a burden to my husband. I smiled at church on Sunday, but I lived daily in a weakened state. Because my heart was fragile, and my soul was worn, my leading worship at my church on Sunday mornings would cause me to have to rest for the remainder of the week.

Many times my husband would ask me to stay home and rest, but staying connected to my faith was the only way I kept my sanity. Have you ever felt like *everything* had been taken from you? That's how I felt. I had lost the career that I loved and was great at doing. I had lost my independence. My husband and I had spent a small fortune on producing my own record label, developing a brand, along with marketing and distributing my music worldwide. I had lost my ability to tour and promote the album I had just recorded. I lost my joy and my will to live. On days when I could not seem to stop crying, I would stand in the shower with the water on, hoping my family would not hear my gut-wrenching sobs. I had come to the end of my rope, and I began to ask God to just let me die.

I know my husband was praying for me. He would many times sit on the side of the bed and tell me that I had to live because there was something great I was supposed to do in the world. Many times, he shared with me inspirational books and powerful sermons. He recorded shows he had discovered that he felt would bring me inspiration! On one such day, he called me upstairs to watch an interview Oprah Winfrey was having with LL Cool J. As I was listening to the interview, I heard LL Cool J say, "Dreams don't have deadlines." His words leaped in me! I rewound the segment and listened to him say it again! Then again and again! In that moment, my inner compass was reset. This was the revelation I needed to begin to break out of a more than six year depression.

I immediately grabbed my iPhone and recorded the quote in my voice memo pad. I realized that the life I was living was not me. I realized that the titles, positions, and multiple awards that I had earned, were not *me*. My ability to sing (or to perform in any way) was not the totality of who I was.

Even though I had been diagnosed with many conditions, I still had power. I could not control everything in life, but I could control my attitude and outlook. I could still push forward with the dreams I had by taking simple, easy, baby steps. That day was the day that I began to want to live again. I could breathe more deeply, and the focus for my true destiny was conceived and began to spring forth. That simple one-liner from LL Cool J became the catalyst for pushing me out of a "stuck place."

I believe that my true calling is to help people around the world get a revelation that life is much like a song. Each of us will experience expected and unexpected movement, highs, lows, rhythms, melodies, and more. With our decisions, actions, and confession we can decide what the lyrics of our lives will be. The simple keys I will share in this book will help you to discover your true inner voice!

I had placed all of my confidence in my natural voice and had been blinded to the fact that *all* of me needed to be developed in order for me to live a consistent, holistic, fulfilled life. *Life Is Your Song: Discover Your Voice* was written to help others see what I now see. Each of us must find our own way to make our voices heard in this world. Staying in a relationship that does not fulfill you, remaining in a job that you hate, taking continual abuse from a person you love, or letting fear keep you from following your dreams is just like placing your hand over your own mouth and refusing to be heard in this world.

Listen! Unless we all live a life of purpose, we are just like a symphony with *no sound*. We have the potential to make beautiful music, but instead we go through the motions of life–never really living! In the pages to follow, I will share with you the amazing things I learned along my journey. What a difference one revelation makes!

Life for me now is like a springtime song in perfect harmony! Soothing melodies linger in my soul. Every moment, new stanzas are written to document God's design for my life. Understanding that our lives are largely mental and emotional, your life can be drastically different the moment you get the revelation that unlocks the prison doors that have bound you! No longer do you have to accept one choice from a cadre of all bad choices. I have the personal power to decide that I want none of those. I chose life. I chose peace. I chose serenity. You can do the same thing. Take these words of wisdom to heart. Your life is your song! Make it a *masterpiece!* Own it–love it–discover it! In the next chapter, I will share with you how I reset my inner compass. Read on!

One

Reset Your Inner Compass

The day that I heard LL Cool J say, "Dreams don't have deadlines," was the day I begin to reset my inner compass. See, I was bogged down with darkness and depression because I could not let go of what and who I thought I was supposed to be. Over and over, I saw glimpses from God that He was going to use my life in a more powerful way, but I just could not mentally accept what was happening to me and how my life had turned out up to that point.

In other words, I really held myself in captivity for more than six years because I was stuck on things having to happen a certain way. The day I realized I could "do something" no matter how small, to change my life, was the day I was freed! You must make a decision that life will no longer happen to you. You will take complete charge of your day and your life!

Too many of us are too reactionary. We wait until something negative happens to us, and then we try to determine how to respond. Before we can react to that negative situation, we are hit by something else. Life, then, becomes a series of us trying to get back up, get our balance, and swing back *after* being hit. This allows us no time to be proactive. During periods like this, our thinking often becomes cloudy and confused.

This book will offer you ways to break out of this type of a vicious cycle. First, you must believe that a better life for *you* is possible. Then, it grows to believing that a *much* better life is *probable*. Today, you will take charge and start impacting your world. Here are ten ways to reset your inner compass, which is your God-given destiny button, within you! Yes, you already have what it takes. Use it.

1

#Reboot

Be confident in the fact that no problem you are facing or challenge you are having is fixed forever! In this life, very few things are permanent–even though our minds like us to believe otherwise. You can simply step back. Look at the situation, and then envision how you would like that situation to look. Take the time to sketch it out, add color to it, give life to what you would like to see happen. Then create that reality in your mind to the degree that it is real to you, even if no one else sees what you see.

If you are dealing with failing health, put up a picture of yourself when you were healthy and vibrant! What you continually visualize, you will eventually become. It probably will not be easy, but it is costing you too much to remain where you are. Work on your mind before you do anything else. It is the most critical organ in your body.

Stop adding to the problem with your words and responses. Turn your inner computer off by refusing to entertain conversations and thoughts that keep you in a loop and start fresh. Control what goes into your eyes, ears, and imagination. There is a reason for your life. Once you find it, peace will flood your existence, and you will not want to return to the old way. It's time to start fresh. It's time to reboot.

Here are five actions I will take to reboot my life today.

_____

_____

_____

_____

_____

2

#Change

Understand that you hold the keys to your own destiny. No person or pain is strong enough to hinder your progress if you decide you want something better for yourself. Decide on a single goal, and determine that you will pay the price to get there. Get to the heart of the matter by studying your past and recognizing what has always held your progress up. Winners get up early and stay up late. Winners do what is "too much" to the average person. Winners anticipate and initiate change.

Embrace the power of *change* on the inside and then things will *change* on the outside. Did you know that change is often designed to separate champions from losers? A loser has a certain pattern of actions programed in his/her mind, and he or she only plans how to respond if things happen that way. Highly successful people plan how they will respond in the face of challenging situations.

Say to yourself, "Change is good for me, and it makes my life better." You have the capacity to adjust seamlessly and quickly. Positive change profits you every time. Soon you will begin to watch for and accept change with excitement and great peace! Embrace change.

Here are five actions I will take to change my life today.

_____

_____

_____

_____

_____

_____

_____

_____

_____

_____

_____

_____

_____

_____

_____

_____

_____

_____

_____

_____

_____

_____

_____

_____

_____

_____

_____

_____

_____

_____

_____

_____

_____

_____

3

#Trust

Begin to rest in the fact that you were created by a Creator who wants the very best for you. Even if you have been deeply wounded, abused, or cast aside, your life is not over. Just know that you are here on this earth for a purpose. You are the creator of your own world, and you frame your world with your personal belief system and the words you speak on a consistent basis. So get up and make your world a breath of fresh air for all to experience. There is always hope beyond the pain. There is always joy on the other side of the tears. Your everyday assignment is to find the "prosperous side" of life. In trusting again, you will realize a deeper level of personal freedom.

Here are five actions I will take to begin to trust again today

_____

_____

_____

_____

_____

_____

_____

_____

_____

_____

_____

_____

_____

_____

_____

_____

4

#Stop

Look at where your inner GPS has taken you, and then decide where you want to go. Determining where you want to go, usually, begins with stopping and remaining stationary for a time. Some people never place their lives on the predetermined paths for themselves because they never take the time to stop. We find ourselves tired and utterly exhausted, but when we look at our actual progress from where we began, we are disappointed. Stopping to contemplate should be the order of business when we are not manifesting the type of results that satisfy the soul. Continuing to be "busy" is not a practice of a highly accomplished person.

If you are allowing someone else to set your destination code, take that power away from that person. As long as you allow others to decide what is best for you, you will continue going in a direction you do not want to go. Something destructive happens inside your very being when you give away power that you should be directing yourself. Don't allow yourself to let your life pass on into eternity and you never sit in the driver's seat. Life is too short. Stop, reassess your life today.

Here are five ways I will stop being busy with things that do not profit me.

_____

_____

_____

_____

_____

_____

_____

5

#Recognize

Accept the fact that much of what you hate about your life is because of your own personal confession and actions. Your words are so powerful that they can cause life or death. Words are vehicles that actually carry you into your next season. I do not speak what I see; I speak what I desire. I envision it. I pay the price to go to my desired destination.

Words are vehicles. Chose them and use them wisely. Once you realize this, you can begin to make the adjustments in your conversations within and without needed for a better life. The quality of your words has everything to do with your future. No longer blame others for the life you are living. If you change what you say and what you do, you can change how you live. I've done it, and you can too!

Below create five positive personal confessions to say aloud each day!

_____

_____

_____

_____

_____

_____

_____

_____

_____

_____

_____

_____

_____

_____

6

#Think

Many people would rather have others think for them because somehow they have reduced their standard to believe that someone else knows what is best for them. Use the brilliant brain that you have been given to analyze yourself and your actions instead of focusing on what others should be doing. Spend dedicated time designing your own life. Solve the problems in your life before you try to fix what is wrong for and in others.

You are smart, capable, and gifted. You have been endowed with a gift, talent, or a skill that is designed to make your name great. You are a champion! Explore ways that you can respond to life and its challenges better.

Here are five ways in which I will use my brainpower to develop strategies that will advance my life.

_____

_____

_____

_____

_____

_____

_____

_____

_____

_____

_____

_____

7

#Write

Journaling is a proven technique to help one release and reflect. Write as though no one will ever read these thoughts, but you. Write down your thoughts, uncensored and without the fear of judgment. After all, they are your thoughts. By owning thoughts through journaling, you can determine if they are worthy to remain in your head after they are reduced to paper, or if you should dispose of them forever.

In your writing, also write down where you want to go in life. What healthy emotional, spiritual, and financial place do you want to live? Write it down, read it daily, take action steps toward your desired goal, and you will achieve it! You act as an architect and an interior designer of your life by journaling. Put it on paper today, and free your mind of having to store every thought that comes to you. Journaling is *powerful*.

Here are five positive thoughts I will write down and mediate on daily.

_____
_____
_____
_____
_____
_____
_____
_____
_____
_____
_____
_____
_____

8

#Create

Did you know that an intricate portion of your assignment as a creation of God is to become a creator of your own world? There is something that happens inside when your creative "juices" are allowed to flow uninhibited. Make a quality decision today that you will spend more time creating and inventing than you will being sad, having pity parties, fussing, fighting, and putting out fires.

Look around you, envision what you desire, create it today. There is a creative spirit that lives within you, do not suppress it. Let the Creator in you live! Let it flow.

Here are five actions I will take to create something new in my life today.

_____
_____
_____
_____
_____
_____
_____
_____
_____
_____
_____
_____
_____
_____
_____
_____

9

#Live

Don't do life or let life happen to you. Live and love life. We must fully understand that a life starts with minutes and moments. Refuse to allow your "moments" to be taken from you. So often, anger, frustration, and circumstances keep us in a continual cycle of seemingly maintaining. Get off of every emotional merry-go-round. If the "pusher" of the merry-go-round will not stop pushing, jump off *now*. Stabilize. Then you can live an "abundant life."

Here are five actions I will take to end the negative cycles in my life.

_____

_____

_____

_____

_____

_____

_____

_____

_____

_____

_____

_____

_____

_____

_____

_____

_____

_____

10

#Reclaim

Reclaim means: **to bring into or return to a suitable condition; to bring back to a right or proper course.**

Your existence was not haphazard. It does not matter how you were conceived or how you got here, your primary assignment is to discern the purpose for which you were created. Then, make an intentional effort to remain in activities and an appropriate environment to nurture your gifts and talents. Your gift to the world is your ultimate contribution to the planet. How do you want to be remembered? What type of legacy do you want to leave behind on this earth? When your name is called, what is the one word that arises in your mind as it relates to your name.

It is time to dig your heels in and get back to the original purpose for your existence. Your life matters. No one else will recognize that fact until you recognize it enough to hone your skills and develop them to the best of your ability. Just like your thumbprint is the only one on the planet, your ultimate contribution to the universe cannot be duplicated. There is only one *you*, and if you prematurely leave this earth, a void will be created.

Take your life back. Take your caring, loving, nurturing personality back. No one has the right to control your emotions or how you feel about yourself and your world except you. So you do not fit into their group, for whatever reason, you do not need their group. Be bold, fierce, and refuse to do anything that does not help others and fulfill you! Be *you*! Be great! Greatness is in your DNA. It's time to let your voice be heard!

Here are five actions I will take to develop my natural gifts.

Two

Understand Your
"True" Identity

Once you have reset your inner compass, you must move to understanding who you really are and then begin living life from the inside out. One of the worst things that can happen to any of us is to lose our inner voice, our true identity. Not being able to speak can greatly affect your life, career, and future. Each of us has, at some time or another, allowed life and all the pain it can bring to make us lose the true essence of who we are and who we were destined to become. Many times, we do not speak out because of the fear of a consequence that we do not want to face.

On the other hand, some are embarrassed to be their true self because they already know that their opinions are in the minority, and they fear judgment or, worse, retaliation. So they remain silent and allow others to determine their path and destiny.

We are three parts: body, soul, and spirit. The spirit, when exposed to prolonged trauma, becomes broken. Once one's spirit has been cracked and destroyed, there is no possible way that person can live the life intended for them. The primary focus then must be placed on being healed and recovering so you can recover your life.

Just like an orchestra has sheet music that tells it what to play, the tempo, movement, and tone, we too must have a guide to finding our path and instructions of how to remain on it. One of the most interesting things about a professional orchestra company is the finesse and simple, elegant smoothness by which the conductor directs all of the sections of the orchestra.

No one instrumentalist is so enthralled in the playing of his own instrument that he does not keep an eye on the direction of the conductor. All notes, tones, and melodies are designed to synchronize in the most harmonious way. Before we can reestablish our identity and live our best selves, the following tips are important to understand and complete.

1. First, our life's song is our personal mission statement. Stop now and write out your personal mission statement. Writing your personal mission statement should not be an overwhelming task. I want to share with you some of the top Foundations and Fortune 500 companies mission statements. See how they were able to put into words what their missions are in twenty five words or less!

Wounded Warrior Project: To honor and empower wounded warriors. (Six words)

CARE: To serve individuals and families in the poorest communities in the world. (Twelve words)

Environmental Defense Fund: To preserve the natural systems on which all life depends. (Ten words)

Public Broadcasting System (PBS): To create content that educates, informs, and inspires. (Eight words)

American Heart Association: To build healthier lives, free of cardiovascular diseases and stroke. (Ten words)

March of Dimes: We help moms have full-term pregnancies and research the problems that threaten the health of babies. (Sixteen words)

American Diabetes Association: To prevent and cure diabetes and to improve the lives of all people affected by diabetes. (Sixteen words)

In Touch Ministries: To lead people worldwide into a growing relationship with Jesus Christ and to strengthen the local church. (Seventeen words)

Save the Children: To inspire breakthroughs in the way the world treats children and to achieve immediate and lasting change in their lives. (Twenty words)

Tonya Ware - Born to help people around the world reset their inner compass, understand who they really are, and find their place in the world. (Twenty-three words)

2. Next, take inventory of what you have in your life already that will help you to complete your personal mission statement. For an example: I am a singer, teacher, communicator, performer, writer, planner, organizer, and more. If I explore all the things I can do with these gifts, the sky isn't even the limit. Discover yourself and you will find your voice and establish your true identity.

3. Then, find successful (productive, balanced, charitable) people from whom you can learn. Fuel your passion by spending time with those who possess a like passion. Before choosing a mentor, ascertain if where they are in life is where you want to be. If spending personal time with them is not possible, purchase their books, CDs, DVDs, and downloads. Hear them live as often as you can. The secret here is to learn how they think, process, and perform. Then use that pattern as a model.

4. Finally, each day put at least five things into action that will cultivate your life's song (which is your personal mission statement). Remember, you do not know something unless you are doing it. Hearing without doing produces no fruit. Strategize on how you can impact and motivate others. Once your focus begins to add value to someone else's life, your own personal challenges shrink. To follow are the five ways I tapped into my true identity and found my inner voice again. Use these keys—they will transform your life.

1

#Pray

Take a few moments throughout your day to pause and pray. Prayer should not be considered a religious activity. Rather, it should be a part of a successful holistic lifestyle. Prayer will help you become more centered. Keep in mind, when you sincerely ask a question, you should expect answers. When you start to expect precise answers, precise answers will appear!

Prayer is my vehicle to get back to the conversation God had with me when I was in spirit form. Access God's mind and plan for your life when you pray—not flowery words and eloquent speech, just talking to the one who created you, from your heart. So take time to pray and then sit quietly as wisdom begins to come to you.

Here are five topics I will begin to pray about.

_____
_____
_____
_____
_____
_____
_____
_____
_____
_____
_____
_____
_____
_____
_____

2

#Build

Acknowledge the good and positive foundations in your life and build on them. If you were fortunate to have parents, a teacher, a friend, or loved ones who gave you a foundation in faith, family, work ethic, or service, *build* on what they have taught you. Do something great with what you have been given.

Here are five ways in which I will build on the good foundations given to me by others.

_____

_____

_____

_____

_____

_____

_____

_____

_____

_____

_____

_____

_____

_____

_____

_____

_____

_____

_____

_____

3

#Dream

Dreaming is fuel to a successful life. Dreaming grants you an escape from what is to what can be. What if you spent the first thirty minutes of your day dreaming about the life you desire? What if you spent time living in that dream for those moments to the point that the dream became more real to you than your current physical reality?

While you are wide awake, listen to music, speakers, and read books that stir your passion to believe your dreams can and will come true. Your dreams fuel your passion. Make it a priority to cultivate and stir dreams in those around you. Once you begin to dream about your bright future, your "failure nightmares" will fade away.

Here are five desires I will dream about today.

_____

_____

_____

_____

_____

_____

_____

_____

_____

_____

_____

_____

_____

_____

4

#Watch

Be observant. Be sensitive to your own actions and others. Don't tolerate foolishness from yourself, and don't accept it from others. Be mindful to treat others as you want to be treated. Love the way you want to be loved. And please do not miss any opportunity to enhance someone's life. As you are generous to those in your close proximity, the universe widens that proximity and places people in your life who have more than you have. Those people will reciprocate what you have endowed upon others.

Be watchful. Be on the lookout for ways to nurture those around you. Watch for the manifestation of your hopes and dreams. They will come to pass.

Here are five ways in which I will be more attentive to things and people in my life.

_____
_____
_____
_____
_____
_____
_____
_____
_____
_____
_____
_____

5

#Forgive

One of the most difficult things you will, most likely, ever do is to forgive others as well as yourself. But there is no possible way that you can find your "real" self and discover your voice if you hold unforgiveness in your heart. Unforgiveness will stifle your creativity and cancel your progress. Even if you were being ushered into greatness, unforgiveness would blind your eyes, and you will not be able to perceive what is right in front of you.

The effects of unforgiveness go deep. It can literally stop you in your tracks. We forgive to set ourselves free. Decide to forgive, regardless of what others do. It is the gift that you give yourself. Forgive and advance. When we chose not to forgive, we are then forced to take the offender everywhere we go. Since you do not want the person who hurt you in your wealthy place, you cannot go either! In letting go, your spirit will begin to soar. Your focus will become what you can become and how you can inspire others. Again, forgive and let go.

Here are five people I will forgive today.

_____

_____

_____

_____

_____

_____

_____

_____

_____

_____

Three

Find Your Place in
the World

Once you reset your inner compass and connect to your authentic life's purpose-your true identity, you must then find the place where you can do the most good for the benefit of the world. In your rightful predetermined position, you will obtain a rhythm to life that will bring you much joy. I am talking about an inner "well" of peace that will ultimately pass all understanding.

While I have never personally experienced it, I have been told that one of the most painful things that a person can experience is a dislocated joint. A dislocated joint renders the person incapable of doing anything except focusing on that intense, excruciating pain. Many times, we live our lives like a joint out of socket. We exist, but everything is colored by that pain that has taken all of our thoughts and focus. In such a situation, everything we do and everything we experience tends to bring us more pain than peace and happiness. Our lives become unbearably uncomfortable, and we hurt more deeply every time our minds are riveted back to that experience.

I had to realize that there where many places in the world where I could be doing something positive. I had to learn to be bold enough to inject myself into places where I could live and operate in my best, highest self.

I am now on a pathway to discover all the places and people I was created to impact. This ensures I will be gladly accepted and celebrated. There is nothing quite as amazing as being in the place where your soul is satisfied. There you will find life that flows with ease! Here are ten keys I am using to find my place in the world. There is nothing greater than living in your own unique flow.

1

#Serve

We all know the universal principle that teaches, "Whatever you sow, you shall also reap." The most potent cure for sadness and self-pity is serving others. Seeing the immediate needs of others illuminates the fact that your life is not so hopeless after all. Remember, vision turned inward causes depression, but vision turned outward causes change! Looking at only your own faults, weaknesses, frailties, and mistakes will ensure deep depression for an unlimited time. Serving others has its strength in giving you an opportunity to turn your attention from yourself.

Look around you and find a worthy cause to support. Roll up your sleeves and stop obsessing over yourself. Intentionally, be for someone else what you believe you need for yourself. Serve and watch your life open up to great opportunities! Give, help, serve, and become a person who cares. Allowing love and kindness to flow toward someone else will heal you as it flows out of you. What you desire to receive must pass through your hands first—*serve*!

Here are five ways in which I will serve my community beginning today.

_____

_____

_____

_____

_____

2

#Meditate

It is true that you will always move toward your *most* dominant thought. While there are many opinions on methods for meditation, all schools agree that mediation is necessary for the calming of the soul and the centering of the mind. Meditation should be a prepared part of your day—preferably at the beginning of your day.

I said it should be a prepared part your day because, if you were programming a computer, you would spend time studying which software, programs, and other information you needed to put into the computer in order for the computer to be equipped to give you the results that you were expecting. The same rule applies as it relates to meditation. You need to know what you are attempting to produce before you input any information.

Too many people enter the day without any mental preparation. They rush into their offices a minute before clock-in time and hope they will have a good day. This is my recommendation. Spend time each day speaking your desired result. Then visualize. Spend equal time quieting your soul. Rid yourself of the negative thoughts when you clear your mind. Meditate on positive confessions, meaningful scriptures, inspiring quotes, and desirable images. You will gravitate toward your daily meditations.

Here are five things I will meditate on each day.

_____

_____

_____

_____

3

#Accept

Accept and love yourself just as you are. This does not mean that you are happy with every aspect of your life. Neither does it mean that you must settle for life as it now is. Accepting and loving yourself removes judgment that ultimately slows you to the place that you are almost immobile. Nothing is worse than judging yourself to the point that all of your efforts are cancelled due to your low self-esteem. Know that you do not have to accept just anything! Your standards protect you from people entering your life who will bring you down.

When you have high expectations of yourself, be careful about who you allow around you. The quickest way to get your passion neutralized is to get toxic people around you. Accepting people into your circle that mock your standards is like tying an anchor around your neck, you will eventually be pulled down.   Accept yourself fully—even though you see things that need to be changed. You cannot love others until you really love yourself. Talk to yourself. Tell yourself you are fearfully and wonderfully made. You are favored. You are empowered to prosper. Seek ways to improve yourself. Give your very best and expect the best! Acceptance is a principle that clears you of critiquing everything. Finally, you can look at yourself and others without an eye to fix or repair. This makes getting better more enjoyable.

Here are five ways I will be more accepting of others and myself.

_____

_____

_____

_____

_____

4

#Reject

Resist and violently reject the temptation to look back. Looking back even for a second can slow your progress. Drive with force and with focus into your future. Get up early and stay up late if necessary to position yourself to win by refusing to accept anything less than five-star excellence! Send back every fear package that arrives at your door. Look forward, think forward, and live forward. Then and only then will all of the entities of your life truly advance.

Here are five things I will no longer allow in my life.

_____

_____

_____

_____

_____

_____

_____

_____

_____

_____

_____

_____

_____

_____

_____

_____

_____

_____

_____

5

#Anticipate

Expect things to be different and better. Anticipation is the Siamese twin to hope. Without the anticipation of good, the enemies of fear, worry, and anxiety will creep in and occupy mental and emotional space that you need to provide optimum fuel for your journey. Be open to new possibilities, but do not allow people who act as though they love you to box you into a situation in which you cannot thrive and be happy. In other words, do not sign a lease to live anywhere that violates your standards.

Instead of fearing that you will lose, anticipate you will win. Today, make a once and for all decision to believe in yourself. Believe in your strengths, your abilities, and your God-given gifts. Trust that the King of the universe sent you into your mother's womb well equipped and properly endowed to complete in excellence your assignments. You are gifted above your imagination.

So, anticipate that you will get the promotion, the opportunity, or the job. But most of all, anticipate the moves *you* will need to make to bring you closer to your goal. Don't procrastinate—anticipate!

Here are five projects I will get moving or involved in starting today.

_____

_____

_____

_____

_____

_____

6

#Close

To move forward, you will have to close the door on the past. Your future is a much better prize than holding on to the defeats of yesterday. The mistakes of your past bought and delivered you an education that no one can take from you. If you have done your inner work and have removed the emotion from the mistakes of your past, you have now conquered that thing—whatever it is.

You are bigger than that experience, and as long as you remain positive and upwardly mobile, you will never be ruled by that thing again as long as you live. Even if it rears its ugly head and rises up to face you again, if you remember the lesson you learned, you can always win. You will have to stop feeding the things in your life that have held you back. Spend your time energizing your passion by looking at the things that are ahead. Greater is coming. Closing doors on the past makes way for better doors opening in your present that will escort you into your glorious future.

Here are five emotional doors I will close and continue to close on today.

_____

_____

_____

_____

_____

_____

_____

_____

7

#Cry

Sometimes you need a "good" cry to get to the next level in life. A "good" cry does not end in depression, but in hope. Once you release all the hurt, let it go. All of us have been wounded, mistreated, and betrayed. Cry about it, and then move on. It has been said that crying purges the soul. Crying in ancient times often meant to grieve for a death. That grieving was for a specific period. Once that grieving period was done, the person or the nation would get up and go on their way.

The best way to move on is by refusing to talk about the person, the situation, or the pain. The power of words is one of the greatest in the universe. Words invoke images and images invoke feelings. Therefore, your first assignment is to stop talking about it. Once you have mastered your conversations, your thoughts will follow, and you will soon stop thinking about it. Once the thing leaves your thought life, it has been removed from your soul. Anytime a negative situation is purged from your soul, your tears will turn in to laughter!

Here are five things I will no longer cry or talk about.

_____
_____
_____
_____
_____
_____
_____
_____
_____

8

#Laugh

Laughter is such an integral part of developing your life's song because laughter is like the power on button on your computer. There are times when even the best of computers have a screen freeze. In the same manner that a computer gets frozen, so can a person if he or she does not engage in active laughter. Laughter "unfreezes" your soul and releases you to move on to the next task that will advance your life.

People who can freely laugh are happy people. Happy people with a mission are productive people. Productive people rule the world. They have mastered grief, sadness, and the temptation to live in the past. Most of all, they are open to new possibilities. Watch a comedy, play with your children, or do something that brings joy to your soul. The reason laughter is like medicine is because—for the moments you decide to laugh—you have also decided not to worry, fret, fear, or cry. Laugh today and every day. You will add years to your life and joy to your heart. Chose to laugh and enjoy your life.

Here are five things that make me happy and stir in me laughter and joy.

_____

_____

_____

_____

_____

_____

_____

_____

9

#Dance

Any body in motion will thrive. If a lake, river, or stream stops moving, it will become stagnant. After a river becomes stagnant, it will soon breed death. When waters are stagnant, the primary thing that happens is that the oxygen supply becomes limited. Without oxygen, life in any form is limited and cannot continue to live and multiply. Your body is the same. When you move your body in dance, you free yourself in the moment. Dance. Your dance may encourage someone else to dance. You will begin to feel more and more like your best self.

Here are five ways I will get my body and mind moving on today.

_____

_____

_____

_____

_____

_____

_____

_____

_____

_____

_____

_____

_____

_____

_____

_____

_____

10

#Sing

Have you ever dealt with a grieving heart that nothing seemed to cure? Sing a song and watch that sadness melt and vanish from your life in an instant. There is something about an uplifting song that helps you to "move on." Singing releases something in people that nothing else can. Find an inspiring song, and sing it as loudly as you can. Don't worry about how it sounds, or if you are singing it just right. It is not the perfecting of the notes or the tune that brings results when you're singing for your own personal therapy.

It is the fact that you allow yourself to become lost in the song. For that moment, nothing else matters! Sing and watch your life start to produce. Sing and watch depression end. Sing and watch your heart be filled with gratitude. Life is your song, discover your voice, and sing! Give expression in the earth that will make a lasting positive effect on others!

Here are my five top songs to sing each day to stir joy within.

_____

_____

_____

_____

_____

_____

_____

_____

_____

_____

_____

Your Life's Lyrics

I encourage you to consider the lyrics you want in your life's song. Do you want people to know you by your kindness, patience, generosity, happy disposition, grace, etc. Each time we show someone "good will" a positive lyric is written about us. Each time we cause hurt or pain to another, a sad lyric is written in our life's story.

Just likes lyrics to a song tell us what's on the heart of the composer, our actions write our stories, and the world reads them. My hope is that you will, like me, chose to make the best out of what you have been given. We may fall and stumble along the way. We may encounter a hardship or a challenge, but we can still live. Get back to what makes you happy. Do all you can to fill your days with things you love. Life is *your* song, discover your voice, and live life to the fullest!

The Speaker

Tonya Ware's heartfelt message, "Life is Your Song: Discover Your Voice" is a moving story everyone experience! Her powerful delivery excites and impacts every audience! Book Tonya Ware for any of the following events.

- Keynote Speaker for Your Conference or Event
- Half-day and Full-day Workshop/Seminar
- Executive and Personal Retreats

Book Tonya Ware Today!

Tonya Ware shares easy to follow tips on how to:
REBOOT your life and start fresh.
CREATE the life you desire.
ACTIVATE the power of being observant.
CLOSE the door on the past and MORE.........

The Coach

My personal coaching involves the ability to understand the real you: I seek to understand how you think, and understand your perspective. Once this has been established, I will provide a new "fresh" viewpoint — expanding and growing you to see a more meaningful and empowering way of life. As a certified Quantum Leap Member, I can see what you are going through now and help you develop into the person who desire to be. Coaching is design to give you an expert who comes alongside you while helping you achieve your goals and overcome your limits or hinderances.

I offer two levels of coaching support:
Individual Coaching — one on one private and confidential coaching

When I am working with you one-on-one, it is my objective to assist you in reaching your purpose, vision and goals by working through the same techniques I used to rediscover my life! Together, we will develop a strategy for you to move your life forward through weekly interaction and accountability.

Group Coaching — small setting onsite

Having the support of others as you work toward becoming your best in life, is so energizing! The bond that is formed enhances each person to develop the authentic person within and share their dreams and passions in a safe environment that nurtures the whole group. Group Coaching is an amazing experience unlike any other.

Please contact me, and together we'll develop an effective plan to move your life forward.

Here's what people are saying about Tonya Ware's Coaching Program:

Before understanding the principles shared by Tonya Ware, my life was lacking purpose. She helped me realize my passion. Now, I am complete. Kim Bracey, Executive - City of Jackson

Before being introduced to the easy to understand wisdom shared by Tonya Ware, I was unemployed. My life was at a stand still. I was born with many talents, yet I was spinning my wheels. Now I see how to be who I was created to be. I am living the dreams that I used to only see while I was asleep. Ty Patterson, Administrator - The Salvation Army

Individual Coaching can be completed via phone conference and/ or Skype.

Tonya Hairston Ware

Biography

T onya H. Ware was born to parents who traveled throughout the
United States, pioneering and planting churches. Tonya began
singing at a young age. After graduating from high school, she enrolled
in and graduated from Mississippi State University. Through voice les-
sons and participating in choir, she acquired pertinent knowledge in
understanding the mechanics of voice. Her voice matured into one that
would inspire many. By the time she graduated from college, her gift of
singing had touched thousands of people all over the world.

In 1997, Tonya and her husband, Bishop Adrian D. Ware, pioneered
The Church Triumphant Global, where she also serves as executive pastor. In addition, Tonya focused on her secular work and for
twelve years was a benefits and retirement planner for a Fortune 500
company. She remained devoted to both spiritual and secular work
for many years, and as musical director at her local church, she has
touched thousands through her gift of song.

In December of 2006, Tonya completed her first recorded work. She
wrote five of the songs, making her both singer and songwriter on

her self-titled debut album, *Tonya Ware—The Voice*. While this CD was originally recorded as urban inspirational, *Tonya Ware—The Voice* crossed over to adult contemporary and soul radio. Tonya continues to create a buzz in the music industry. Her debut CD, *Tonya Ware—The Voice*, has people all over the world taking notice of her talent.

Tonya's passionate single release, "Put My Hand in Yours," written by Marvin Winans, stands up to some of today's "hottest" music—both in mainstream and Christian markets. The production and sound quality are second to none. Her music video for "Put My Hand in Yours" has been featured on *BET*'s "Video Gospel," *Music Choice, Blastro, The Word Network* and more. She has also been featured on the *Gospel Music Channel*. Her voice can be heard around the world on satellite radio.

On July 13, 2008, Tonya was presented with a "Jackie" Award from the Mississippi Gospel Music Association for National Female Soloist of the Year. Also in 2008, Tonya Ware was recognized as a Billboard New Song Contest Honoree and was a KKCM Songwriter Finalist. Tonya Ware is a 2009 Stellar Award-nominated artist for Contemporary Female Artist of the Year. In 2009, Tonya was presented with another "Jackie" Award from the Mississippi Gospel Music Association.

In 2010, she was named Mississippi president for the Warrior Bride National Prayer Network and was elected in 2012 to the Wisdom Team for the International Congress of Churches and Ministries.

In June 2013, Tonya participated in the Jacobs School of Music's Summer Jazz Vocal Program, moving the audience with her amazing voice. In August 2013, Tonya Ware studied two weeks in Los Angeles in the singer/songwriter program at Berklee School of Music sharpening her skills. While in the Berklee singer/songwriter program, she was awarded a scholarship by Berklee to begin studying online as she continues to inspire audiences with her remarkable voice.

Tonya is the host of "Winning in Life," an inspiring weekly session that she uses to share principles on purpose, health, managing life's challenges, wealth, business, and more. She is the director of Daughters of Wisdom and is active in the community, touching lives in various ways. Most importantly, she is the "lovely wife" of Adrian D. Ware and the proud mother of two beautiful daughters: Wisdom Noelle and Wealth Joy.

www.TonyaWare.com
#LIFEisyoursong